I BELIEVE

within the

CHURCH

I BELIEVE
within the
CHURCH

a personal witness
Bishop Peter J. Cullinane

VERITAS

First published 2006 by
Veritas Publications
7/8 Lower Abbey Street
Dublin 1
Ireland
Email publications@veritas.ie
Website www.veritas.ie

ISBN 1 85390 922 X

A catalogue record for this book
is available from the British Library.

*The references to the scriptures (in italics) are sometimes quotations,
sometimes paraphrases and sometimes only allusions. But in all cases,
they faithfully reflect the meaning of the scripture. Translations are
based on the* New American Bible *(Oxford University Press, 1995),
the* New Jerusalem Bible *(Darton, Longman & Todd Ltd, 1990) and
the* New Revised Standard Version *(Catholic Bible Press, 1993).*

Printed in the Republic of Ireland
by Betaprint Dublin

Veritas books are printed on paper made from the wood pulp
of managed forests. For every tree felled, at least one tree is
planted, thereby renewing natural resources.

CONTENTS

INTRODUCTION:

TOWARDS A CREDO

When we tell others who we are, we give them details about ourselves that help to identify us – our name, where we come from, what we do and so on. We identify ourselves more fully when we explain what is really important to us. For instance, on big occasions some indigenous peoples still recite their genealogy; telling where they belong is part of telling who they are.

Similarly, we declare our identity by reciting what our community believes, i.e. what holds it together as the same community. For example, if I had belonged to one of the ancient Hebrew communities, I would have identified myself by reciting a formula like this:

> My father was a wandering Aramean. He went down into Egypt to find refuge there, few in number; but there he became a nation, great and strong. The Egyptians ill-treated us, but we called on Yahweh the God of our fathers…and Yahweh brought us out of Egypt with a mighty hand and outstretched arm…and with signs and wonders.

He brought us here and gave us this land…Here,
then, I bring the first-fruits of the produce of the
soil that You, Yahweh, have given me.

(Deut. 26:5–10)

For the descendants of Abraham and Sarah, this
wandering Aramean's history was their history too,
and the promises God had made to him were for them
too. They declared who they were by declaring their
history, their faith, their hope and their thanks to God.
That is what a 'Credo' is.

The early Christians declared who they were
through their worship, preaching and scriptures, and of
course, above all, through their lives. Moving out
beyond the frontiers of their Jewish origins, they re-
expressed their faith in fresh and contemporary ways,
using the thought patterns of Roman and Greek culture.
Early in the fourth century, they formulated their faith
in the Creed we recite when we come together for the
great Prayer of Thanksgiving – the Eucharist. United by
what we believe, we say as one 'I believe'. We declare
our history, our faith, our hope and our thanks.

That community's faith, hope and thanksgiving
help me to interpret God's goodness to me. I name it
here in the hope of encouraging others to name and
nurture what God is doing for them.

…a new social reality requires fresh ways of
presenting the faith.

(Pope John Paul II to the Church in Oceania,

para. 22)

PROLOGUE

Faith is confident assurance concerning what we
hope for,
and conviction about things we do not see.

(Heb. 11:1)

The melody of life is its meaning
and a life that isn't sung
isn't lived.
Even pain can't stop a heart singing
music it knows it has heard.
But sometimes it's hard to be sure of what is only
hoped for
and convinced of what no one can see.

Not everyone chooses to sing.

Some see shades and think it is night
but shadows mean the day!
Purpose – even half revealed –
lights up the whole
enough for us to see
that if it were night, even shadows wouldn't be.

And so in the day I see and I sing
though clouds overhead cast shadows where I walk
in fragmented light,
and meaning in glimpses leaves questions still.

But music needs words before it's a song
that others can hear and join in.
Already, before me, a pilgrim people
wends its way through a valley
to a chorus mighty, sure and strong.

Is that my journey, is theirs my song?
Can my heart sing except in their midst
if with them is where I belong?

Yet not for me cacophony;
from clutter I must be free.
I'll walk with them and sing their song,
not for me to change their tune.
But I must know which part is mine;
my song must still be me!

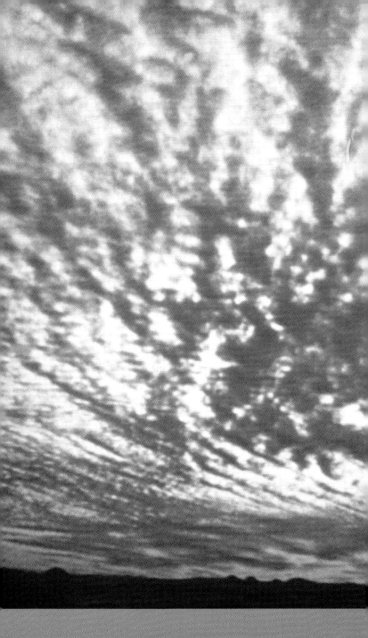

PART I

Who is this, so much at home where children play,
but not yet home,
holding on to what I know, yearning for something
more?
Bathed in sun's warming beams
sinking in the sensuous sand
drowned in the sound of the sea
lost in the infinite blue
gliding through planetary space
all the time by this log, I am here;
it is me.
The flower beside me tells of You.

In the midst of all that might not have been
I am
a choice You didn't have to make:
my all is all gift.
You spoke and I was called
You chose and it was me.
In a sea of gifted existence, especially *when it's still*
and *I am still*,
I find myself in Your presence,
and bow down in adoration.

New ways of searching out the mysteries of your
creation
confirm old ways of knowing that *everything You made
is good*.
Made for us to enjoy, life is good
and so are You.
On the journey into reality
we love You in loving
everything You have made –
each for what it is and nothing for what it's not.
And so I cannot cling to what must pass away.
In both its splendour and its insufficiency,
the world You made points me to You.

You made me for such love as only You can give;
'my heart will find no rest until it rests in You'.
I come to be through being-for-You.
The more I am yours, the more I am me.
I thank You for the *wonder of my being*
and the gift of knowing You.

This same world which leads me to expect more than
it can give
seems unable to tell me what I most need to know.
It cannot tell me that goodness has the last word over
evil
and life over death.
I think of broken hearts and people hurt
by loneliness, hunger, fear…
those with nowhere to go and no one to care;
people trapped in illnesses of the mind
or in camps for refugees;
others from whom your gift of life and
their right to live
have been torn away by guns or greed
or clinical termination: the result is the same.
I need to know that love's sacrifices are not all for
nothing
and friendship's joys are forever.
I see the stars and watch the sea and marvel at your
glory;
but centuries ago others looked and they are gone…
someone cried, and we don't know their names.
O God, do You not have something more to say?

Yes, in the silence You have spoken
your *Word became flesh*
and dwelt among us, as Jesus of Nazareth.
What more could You say about yourself, and us,
than You have said in sending him
the visible *image of your unseen self*?
What need for more assurance that You
respond in love to every prayer
who have already given us more than we could ask?
Through your Word made flesh we come to know
that You love what You have made
and *save what You love*.

It is him I see
where the *branches draw life from the vine*.

In the community called Christian,
I find people of flesh and blood and ordinary lives
living in expectation of meeting You,
undefeated by their personal failures and by death
itself.
I have watched their faces in quiet prayer and in songs
of joy;
I have heard their professions of faith and confessions
of failure;
I have felt humbled no less by their repentance than
by their faithfulness;
I have known their sacrifices,
been empowered by their serenity
and learned the reason for the hope that is in them.
Their sureness is not based on any success of their own
but on what they believe You have done for them.

There is power in what they seem to know,
the more because human nature is weak.
I thank You, Father, for having revealed great things to little ones.
In the community of those who live
now not they but Christ living in them,
I have seen frail human nature raised up
reaching heights of hope and depths of peace
which nothing in the world could give, nor take away.
IN THEIR MIDST I COME TO KNOW
THAT HE who enabled the lame to walk and the blind to see
and sinners to start again
IS RISEN,
for that is what their lives proclaim.
And so I believe in him in whom they have placed their trust.

I bless this community in which sinners and saints can
both belong
and which cared enough to claim me
before I could claim it,
so that now I can.
And so I look to this community
in which faith and hope and love reveal *your power at
work in us*
and I ask it to account for what it has first enabled me
to know
through experiencing lives of faith and hope and love.

It began outside an empty tomb, in a garden.
It became a fire, a passion, a people.
The new covenant in his blood,
exceeding that of a thousand years before,
created a *chosen race, a royal priesthood,*
a consecrated nation, a people set apart,
called out of darkness into your wonderful light
where it's possible to see and name
the marvellous things
You have done and are doing
for the salvation of all.

When the sun rose that Sunday morning,
a new day dawned upon our world,
the day that gave all days their light.
He was the *first born of many*
whose destiny was linked with his.
With Peter, John and Mary of Magdala,
I believe
that what was too good to be true, is true;
what was too much to hope for, is ours.
So my heart rejoices, my soul is glad,
and even my body shall rest in hope.
Trusting in You can never be in vain.

Now they knew, now I know,
that evil's greatest hour was its own
undoing.
Life's unfairness no longer needs to be
explained away;
Even our guilt we can own,
for *when we were undeserving*
You loved us still.
On that weekend, my own life
became worthwhile for ever.
Nothing in the *past, present or future*
can come between us and your love
made visible in Jesus Christ our Lord.
Who are we that You
should care so much, or care at all?
What kind of God are You?

Within this community, I come to know
what in the darkness I could not see –
that *the plan You formed long ago*
(before there was any sin)
was to bring everything together
under Christ as head,
everything in the heavens and everything on earth.

The *Word who was with You*
before the world was made
and through whom all things were made,
began his existence as one of us
in the womb of Mary of Nazareth in Galilee.
She *conceived by the power of your Holy Spirit,*
a sign that our salvation could not come
from human stock or will of the flesh,
but only as mercy and grace from *on High.*

After thirty-three years in obscurity
and two-and-a-half years of public life,
He was put to death by crucifixion, by order of
Pontius Pilate,
at Jerusalem, on the eve of the Jewish Passover,
probably Friday 7 April, AD 30.

During his life on earth
he offered up prayer and entreaty, aloud and in silent tears,
to the One who had the power to save him out of death
and he submitted so humbly that his prayer was heard.
Although he was Son,
he learned to obey through suffering;
and having been made perfect, he became for all
who obey him
the source of eternal salvation.
And because *his prayer was heard*
He was raised to life
and with him *the whole of creation,*
as it groans in giving birth
to the fullness of life and joy ahead.

He had reversed what happened
when sin entered the world:

Though his nature was divine
he did not deem equality with You
something to be clung to.
Rather he emptied himself…
and being as we are,
he was humbler yet
even to accepting death,
death on a cross.
Because of this, You raised him high…

You have transformed our human existence
from being in bondage to evil
to being *in solidarity with him*
whom evil cannot bind.
Now even *death has lost its sting.*

What we suffer against our will
You are in the midst of because You choose
to accompany us through
*like the mother who cannot forget
the child of her womb* — no matter what,
no matter where, no matter when.
Even the suffering of our sinfulness
You took to yourself
in him who *knew no sin*
and changed it into glory.
O Mysterious God. O Wonderful God. O Merciful
God!

After his resurrection, he showed himself
to witnesses *chosen in advance.*
From Jerusalem they *went out*
to the ends of the earth
(where they found me)
and later, this is what they said:

> *Blessed be the God and Father of our Lord*
> *Jesus Christ,*
> *who in his great mercy gave us*
> *a new birth to a living hope*
> *through the resurrection of Jesus Christ from the dead*
> *to an inheritance that is imperishable...*
> *kept in heaven for You*
> *who by the power of God are safeguarded*
> *until the salvation prepared is revealed*
> *at the end of time.*
> *This is cause for great joy for You*
> *even though You may for a short time*
> *have to suffer various trials.*
> *Although You have not seen him*
> *You love him*
> *and without seeing him You now believe in him,*
> *and rejoice with an indescribable joy,*
> *touched with glory,*
> *because You are achieving faith's goal,*
> *your salvation.*

In person *He is our peace and reconciliation*:
He is the *new creation, our virtue and justification*.
All these are ours
through union with him
in the power of your Holy Spirit.
This communion of life
his life in us –
becomes a sign to others
of their destiny too.
It is a sign that beckons them
to where *the length and breadth, height and depth*
of your love and wonderful plan
are more fully revealed, more clearly seen.
Yet they, too, of *other faiths and good conscience*
are being saved by him
who died *for all*
and who *alone can save*.

When we cry 'Abba', Father,
your spirit bears witness with our spirit
that we are your children
and joint heirs with your Son.
But it is only as brothers and sisters of each other
that we can call You *our Father.*
In Christ there is neither Jew nor Greek,
slave nor citizen, male nor female.
Your love is the same for all
and is the measure of each person's dignity –
not their usefulness or ability to function,
not their good works or their folly.

Jesus taught the people what it will be like
when *your will is done on earth as in heaven.*
This time was near, even at hand,
because *the joy they experienced in his company*
was already the beginnings of great things to come.
In his presence they knew
beyond their understanding –
that You cared
and they mattered.
He preached what it will be like when your love has
full reign
over all hearts and all creation;
Enough for us to open our hearts to your great
compassion,
and not limit our openness to your unlimited love.

No longer confined by time or place
he walks with us and we with him, as if in Galilee,
where those who got close to him discovered
a person in whose presence they liked to be.
Now so can we.

More reluctantly they learned that they too must
go up with him to Jerusalem,
and *drink his cup*.
We feel the pangs of letting go
of this world's unfinished forms.
Yet they live more fully, and are more free,
who are not afraid to lose all.
Our passover is joined to his
in *the breaking of the bread*.
The acceptable sacrifice of his own life
the price he paid for being faithful –
is made present under the sign of
the Supper he gave *on the night before he died*.
Receiving him, we become the body and blood
given up and poured out for others.

By the power of your Spirit we go
'through him, with him and in him' to You.

Around his table we become the Church – the
community of his disciples
still in his presence, still hearing him speak,
still being called and still being sent;
still *united in prayer*
with Mary the mother of Jesus;
'one body, one spirit, in Christ',
in whom our lives become an acceptable offering to You.

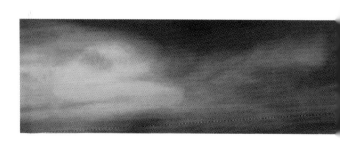

Truly human in mind and heart, body and soul,
and in all his relationships,
he showed us the way
to make human life more truly human,
through opening our lives to You.
Being 'fully human and fully alive
even in troubled waters –
is how we honour You'.

Whatever promotes the life and dignity,
rights and equality of every person
is the continuation of Jesus's ministry
and 'the way the Church must travel';
our way because based on the Incarnation,
yet common ground with all who love humanity.

Our works of love and justice, of creativity and beauty
are the language of life and of setting free.
They are signs of that future
in which we shall 'find once again…
the good fruits of human nature and human enterprise…
     cleansed and transformed'.
Lives with that kind of future matter
and are reasons for wonder.
What shall be holy forever is holy now.

This salvation is pure gift,
not deserved and not earned.
Our good works are your work in us,
fruits of your grace.
Like the *fig tree that didn't bear fruit*,
faith without deeds is dead.

This great communion of love and life
unites heaven and all creation, and is

> manifested in lives that are signs of Christ
> still with us:
> feeding the hungry, visiting the lonely,
> working for peace, dying for justice,
> forgiving and giving hope;
>
> celebrated and nourished in intimate
> moments of meeting:
> in the scriptures, sacraments and prayer;
>
> articulated in teachings that identify what
> his disciples believe;
> and express the meaning of our life *in
> Christ*;
>
> served by a *variety of gifts and all sorts of
> service.*

There is a variety of gifts, but always the same Spirit;
There are different ministries, but always to the same Lord;
working in all sorts of different ways in different people,
it is the same God who is working in all of them.
To each is given the manifestation of the Spirit
for the common good.

In the *household of faith* some are called
to hold authority as a service to others,
appointed by *the laying on of hands*
and the sending of your Spirit
to oversee the Church and *wash the disciples' feet*.
Through them You make visible
the ministry of the Good Shepherd,
who is with us *till the end of time*.

You also make present among us
the ministry of Peter,
whom Jesus *appointed to tend his flock*.
His special role was still being highlighted
and was recorded in the gospels,
even after Peter himself had died.
May we have the courage to be
as Jesus prayed: *one flock under one shepherd*
so that the world could believe
it was You who sent him.

The scriptures, too, were conceived by the power of
your Spirit
and born of the community
in which they were written, proclaimed and
preserved,
and to which we look to be sure of their meaning.
Their interpretation is never just for one's self to decide.
Nor is their meaning the same
as every good purpose they might serve.
Yet through them You speak to each of us personally.

In ministries and sacraments nothing is added to the
work of your Son
and none of his work repeated;
his saving words and deeds
are made PRESENT TO US
for the sake of being received by us:

> it is 'Christ who speaks to us
> when the scriptures are read in the assembly';

> it is Christ who forgives and heals, gives life and
> strength,
> through what is done in his name
> by those he sends in his name;

> above all in the Eucharist
> *it is the Lord*
> who gives his very self
> so that we may be one with him
> in the offering of himself to You
> and in being *given up* and *poured out* for others,
> which is 'the criterion by which to judge
> the authenticity of our Eucharistic
> celebrations'.

In prayer it is not You who change, but ourselves.
When we ask others to intercede for us
it is not as if You need to be persuaded or informed;
but being attracted by the work of
your grace in them,
we become more open to the wonderful things
You already want to do for us.
Drawn to them we are drawn to You,
as others will be by *the life and death of each of us.*

Participating in the community's rituals, memories
and practices,
we are drawn into *the mystery of Christ*
present among us,
away from any ego-spirituality or idealised self
(as if You could be a means to our ends)
into the faith, spirituality and mission
of Jesus' disciples.

I find my true self through being called and sent
to participate in the transformation of all things
through love *that is patient and kind…*
that never seeks its own advantage…or broods over injury,
does not rejoice at wrong-doing, but rejoices in the truth…
is always ready to make allowances,
to trust, to hope and to endure whatever comes.

Because he is *with his church always*
he enables it to *know the way*,
and as it travels the journey, to articulate what it knows
by knowing him.

What is expressed first in lives of faith
is also expressed in prayers, songs, creeds and teachings.
It finds new expression in different times, different
needs and different cultures,
always the same faith.

But the words and symbols we use can never fully
express
the events of our salvation
or the meaning of our *life in Christ*,
for these are always greater
than what we can say or understand.
Doctrines point beyond themselves to him
who is *the way, the truth and the life*.
And so I willingly trust myself to what is proclaimed
in his Church.

I expect the Church's moral awareness to be
subject to the ordinary laws of gradualness and
growth
in how it comes to understand
what it more deeply knows.
But I also expect the truth to be always greater
than my own grasp of it.
And so I am able to let it make demands on me
which may not always coincide with 'where I am'
or how I feel
And so *the truth sets me free*:

> free to know more than I can understand;
> free from being left unsure;
> free to seek the truth yet more;
> free to expand.

But is not the Church's own history also marred by sin?
Have not even its leaders sometimes turned the Good News into bad
by unfaithful lives and repressive ways,
and not always being open to the tradition
of being *open and Catholic*?
Have we not huddled in the boat
when we were called to *walk on water*,
succumbing to timidity, over-caution and convention
when the Gospel required boldness and imagination?

Have we not damaged people's lives
and distorted your image in us
by thinking of male as somehow more
and of You as somehow male?
Have not some too willingly *taken the places of honour*
and wordly titles,
worn broader phylacteries and longer tassles,
been greeted obsequiously and *lorded it over*?
Have we not persecuted the prophets?

But these aberrations cannot last as we become
more open to the meaning of baptism and the
meaning of Eucharist,
and accept that to embody the ministry of Jesus
we must *put on the mind of Christ*.
Union with him is what makes the Church;
deepening our relationship with him
(in the ways that friends do)
is what renews the Church.

Though no explaining can make wrong right,
mercifully your plan is not about us being always
right
or being as we should have been.
It is about what You are doing because we have done
wrong and been unfaithful.
There is no bad news of our making that isn't
swallowed up
in the Good News of what You are doing
beyond our greatest dreams.

If great are the sins by which You are not defeated,
great is the mercy by which You will have your way.

Sin and error in your church only need human
weakness for their explanation;
goodness and love and truth in the midst of such
weakness
need You for their explanation.
And so, believing all the more,
I too ask for mercy
lest the world not realize that He
whose name we bear
was sent by You
to reconcile all things
and that we are ambassadors of this reconciliation,
though we carry this treasure in earthen jars.

Such, then, is the community from which I have sought
an account of the hope that is in it
and the reason for mine.
But perhaps the community which brought me the meaning of my life
is also entitled to expect something from me.
How better to possess the meaning of my life
than by revealing to others the meaning of theirs?
And so I believe that
through the community
in which my faith and hope and love are shaped,
I have been called...

PART II

At the one moment in the whole of history
when uniting sperm and ovum
could have been me
(any other combination would have been someone
else),
You spoke and I came to be.
While gases and dust still swirled about
before the planet was formed and
through every turning point of history and human
free choice,
You guided the universe towards my life,
which later became what You and I would make
together.
What else can it mean to believe that
You are Lord of all history
and of my life too, even as You make me free?

You have never abandoned me, even when You
seemed most absent,
for You entered my life more fully at those times
when *aloud and in silent tears I prayed to the One who
had the power*
to make things different – but didn't,
because You wanted me to choose your will instead
and be more at one with You.

When You allowed me to experience failure and
confusion
it was in order to unmask the falsehood
of self-sufficiency and self-justification,
and make me place all my hope and trust in You.
This is 'passover' and being set free;
this is baptism-being-lived, and life *in the spirit*.

Through the *valley of darkness*, therefore,
You have led me more surely
and enabled me, even *out of the depths*, to thank You
with joy.
I would bless the cross that took me there,
but You already have…

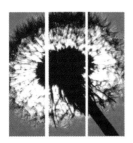

In this pattern of my personal salvation history
I recognise my calling to *reflect in my life*
the pattern of his
who, even though he was Son,
learned obedience through suffering.
Your power was made manifest
in his vulnerability and seeming defeat.
Now, united to him,
when I am weak is when I am strong.

I have felt drawn to him
as others did when they found in him their reason for
living.
I have felt called to be with him also in the loneliness
of his mission
and to give myself for him
who *gave himself up for me.*

The fabric of my vocation has been cut from
the raw materials of an ordinary life and humble
background,
my family and those who loved me before I could
understand
losses and broken hopes,
personal failures and healing grace,
work in the paddocks of Oringi and songs in the cowshed
(where I was happy to be),
centres of learning and far away places,
times of turmoil and trusted friends.

Above all, You have shaped me for ministry to
your people
by their own wonderful faith and prayers, hopes and love
in which You reveal to me
your assurances, your love and your expectations.
Helping them to know how much they mean to You
is the privilege
your call bestows on me.

Being entrusted with their secrets
and faced with their pain, struggles, hopes and joys;
being privy to the mysteries
of your own dealings with them;
discovering that it was Christ they met
in things I said and did in his name,
and finding I have been ministered to
in ministering to them –
these are experiences that surprise, humble and amaze
me –
and confront me with the mystery of my own calling.

If now 'the flower beside me tells of You',
it is because many years ago one who loved her
flowers
told me your name.
I thank You for a grandmother's hand
that led a five-year-old-boy, on frosty mornings,
a mile's walk on a country road
to where we caught a train that took forever
smoke from coal and wooden seats –
so that I could start life with a Catholic education.

It couldn't last, and didn't, but could it be
that long forgotten conversations along that
country road
sowed flowers that still bloom?

And so, standing in *the light of Christ*,
I BELIEVE,
WITHIN THE CHURCH.

May the last word on my life be 'thank You '
for all that has been and all that will be.
And when my life belongs to the distant past
and all our names have been forgotten,
may it be that I –
together with those I loved and those who loved me –
was entrusted by the community called Christian
to the One called Christ.
Grant me the grace to *look forward to his coming again,*
as she surely did who prays for us
'now and at the hour of our death'.

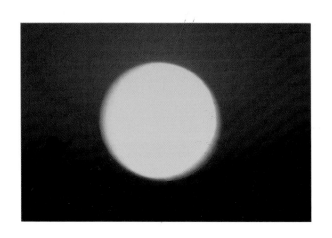

Glory be to You
whose power, working in us,
can do infinitely more than we can ask or
imagine;
glory be to You from generation to generation
in the church
and in Christ Jesus for ever and ever, Amen.

APPENDIX

	1 Corinthians 11:23 ff
	Luke 22:19-20
	Conclusion of Eucharistic Prayer
	Acts 1:14
	Eucharistic Prayer 3
	Romans 12:1
38	cf Iraneus
	Pope John Paul II, The Redeemer of Man, para. 14 & passim
39	Second Vatican Council, Church in Modern World, para. 39 & passim
	Matthew 21:18-22
	James 2:14-16
40	Paul's letters, passim
41	1 Corinthians 12:4 ff
	cf Ephesians 2:19
	2 Timothy 1:6
	John 13:1 ff
	Matthew 28:20
	John 21:15-19
	John 10:16 & 17:23
42	2 Peter 1:20
43	Second Vatican Council, Liturgy, para. 7
	John 20:21
	John 21:7, 1 Corinthians 10:16
	Luke 22: 19-20
	cf Pope John Paul II, Remain with us Lord, para. 28
44	Romans 14:7
45	Colossians 1:27
	1 Corinthians 13:4-7
46	Matthew 28:20
	John 14:6
	2 Timothy 1:1 & St Paul's letters passim
	John 14:5
47	John 8:32
48	Philippians 4:8
	Matthew 14:22-33
	Matthew 23:5-7
	Matthew 23:31-32
	Philippians 2:5
49	2 Corinthians 5:17-20
	2 Corinthians 5:7
50	1 Peter 3:15
53	Hebrews 5:7
	Romans 8:1-17
	Psalm 23:4
	Psalm 131:1
54	Philippians 3:7-11
	Hebrews 5:8
	2 Corinthians 12:9-10
	Galatians 2:20
57	John 8:12
	2 Peter 3:12
	cf the 'Hail Mary'
58	Ephesians 3:20, 21